DRIFT

DRIFT

POEMS

ALAN KING

DETROIT, MICHIGAN

DRIFT

Willow Books
www.WillowLit.com

Willow Books, a Division of Aquarius Press
PO Box 23096
Detroit, MI 48223
www.aquariuspressbookseller.net

Cover photo: Marlene Hawthrone
Cover design: Aquarius Press
Book design: Tony Medina

ISBN 978-0-9852877-0-2

Library of Congress Control Number: 2012932288

ACKNOWLEDGMENTS

Grateful acknowledgment is made to the editors of the following magazines and journals in which some of the poems herein first appeared: *13 Miles from Cleveland, Alehouse, Ampersand, Asterius, Best Poem, Borderline, Boxcar Poetry Review, Breadcrumb Scabs, Clarion, Denver Syntax, The DuPage Valley Review, Edison Literary Review, Farfelu, Farm House Magazine, Ghoti Magazine, Gloom Cupboard, If Poetry Journal, Indiana Review, Lucid Rhythms, Moloch, Moulin Review, Mythium, Naugatuck Review, No Tell Motel, Northville Review, Obsidian, Oranges & Sardines, Perpetual Magazine, Pirene's Fountain Poetry Journal, Prime Numbers, RATTLE, Second Run, Shoots and Vines, Sou'wester, Suisan Valley Review, Umbrella, Vanilla, Welter*

"Invocation" appears in *Full Moon on K Street: Poems about Washington, DC* (Plan B Press, 2009) edited by Kim Roberts.

"Spin Cycle" was nominated for the 2009 "Best of the Net" Selection.

"The Meek" was nominated for the 2009 Pushcart Prize.

Thanks to the centers of learning and institutions of higher education for providing space, resources and refuge, without which the birthing of this book would not have happened: Howard University, Cave Canem Foundation and summer workshop/retreat for African American poets, DC Creative Writing Workshop, Hart Middle School and the Funky Cold Workshop.

I want to thank my mom and dad, Rosalind and Winston King, for supporting my craft the best way they knew how. I have to also thank Tosin, my siblings Alicia and Drew, my aunts, uncles and cousins—all of whom were my first audience. Thanks for listening!

Big thanks to Heather Buchanan, publisher of Aquarius Press/Willow Books and editors Randall Horton and Patricia Biela for publishing this collection. I would like to thank Tony Medina, my teacher and mentor, for the cover idea (and editorial eye) and Marlene Hawthrone for making it happen!

Much gratitude to my other teachers and mentors: Cornelius Eady, Yusef Komunyakaa, Erica Hunt, Cyrus Cassells, Patricia Smith, Toi Derricotte, Ed Roberson, Colleen McElroy, Angela Jackson, Willie Perdomo, and all the great faculty at Cave Canem and VONA.

Shouts to the following friends, fellow poets and all-around good folks: Derrick Weston Brown (my best friend and soon-to-be best man), Fred Joiner (my mellow my man), John Murillo (*UP JUMP THE BOOGIE* is tough!), Truth Thomas (all in God's time), Denise Johnson, Ebony Golden, Melanie Henderson, Ernesto Mercer, Brandon Johnson, Brian Gilmore, Patrick Washington, Bianca Spriggs, John Moody, Venus Thrash, Reginald Dwayne Betts, Kyle Dargan, Holly Bass, Sarah Browning, Kim Roberts, Kimberly Washington, Abdul Ali, Tim Seibles (thanks for taking me under your wing!), Tyehimba Jess (thanks for the liquor at my birthday party!), A. Van Jordan (thanks for even taking a look at my earlier poems!), Katy Richey, Nicole Sealey, Jennifer Steele, Myisha Cherry, Drew "the broke baller" Anderson, Dwayne Lawson, Tim'm West, Ruth Ellen Kocher, DeLana Dameron, Adrian Ayers, Reginald Harris, Teri Cross Davis, Hayes Davis, Darry Strickland, Patricia Spears Jones, Ashaki Jackson, Nancy Schwalb, Amanda Johnston, Dante Micheaux and Shakeema Smalls.

Finally, shout-outs to my Willow Books fam: Curtis Crisler, Derrick Harriell, Lita Hooper, Antoinette Brim, Tara Betts, Rachel Eliza Griffiths, Kelly Norman Ellis, James E. Cherry, Reginald Flood, Samiya Bashir and Parneshia Jones. I'm honored to be in the company of so many shining souls!

CONTENTS

God Light

for Mom

And what's your secret—
more than sermons
and scriptures?

Even when time
gobbles down the weekend
in a gulp and a gang

of workdays eye you
like punks—punching their palms
with a grin and a wink—

there you are
as if the world
weren't a ball of yarn

unraveling in the hands
of toddlers.
You with a Sufi's glow,

with what makes you
interstellar, or celestial,
bright as blessings.

ONE

Spirit of Washington

My brother Drew said the boy
must have smoked it
before screaming and punching a wall
at the back of the movie theater
before gloved hands rushed him with tasers.

Two pulls left Jay naked in the woods
behind our high school, howling
at a milky-white eye in the dark sky.

Was that what made Terrance
lie across double solid lines, then laugh
as a neighbor swerved
to keep from crushing him?

This boat made of rolling paper
and herb dipped in fluid
that preserves dead bodies,
far from a cruise liner
sailing the Potomac.

Cipher

Thought I was wrong
rolling through Adrian's
potluck with Popeye's
and a 2-liter Coke

but the host, in a reefer nod
with others on the front steps,
is too high to care if what I brought
was homemade or from Safeway.

I stood among them a year ago—
everyone, but me, pinching and
pulling from a roach-sized blunt.

The kiss in rotation—more seductive
than greens cooking in the kitchen
and corn roasting on a grill out back.

Not even the spicy aroma
of crispy chicken and butter-
glazed biscuits
could undo this circle
of puff and pass.

Cravings

after Tim Seibles

Follow the trail of bones
and they might lead you
back to a city block
of busted hydrants—

an area scattered with
bodies gnarled like gummi
candies and the licorice
of twisted metal from

uprooted buildings.

When I stomp, streets are
Graham crackers crumbling
under a child's fist. I've chomped
my way, like Pac Man, through

fast food chains; I am

a bi-coastal gopher eating
his way across America,
my brain hijacked by hunger
whose demolition tendencies
send me on a feeding frenzy—

overturning police cruisers,
swatting at helicopters
buzzing around
like dragonflies.

3 a.m.

An hour before, we were lying
in your bed—your fingers trailing
my spine, finding the pool

at the small of my back. I laughed
when you said we'd be a married
couple holding each other

on a night like this—rain drumming
your windows, lightning
shining our slippery bodies;

my calf sore from a charley horse
pulled from what happened earlier.
The night breeze cooled

our bodies. *Will it always be
like this?* you wondered, as if
this was all it took

to keep you here, as if you
wouldn't later lose interest
and move on. All I have is how
we indulged in one appetite

after another—the first, a craving
between bodies, then the other
that brings us to a near empty diner.

Your smile, as I call this
a "late night caper," the only
lit spot on a darkened road.

Revelation

Inside the Uptown Diner,
you watch terror
flash across the gaping face

of a young host
as if the wall of bodies
were closing in on him.

Weren't you as young
when the expectations of others
sent you crouching, looking

for somewhere to hide? You might
have been a lens the way you once
made everything seem larger

than they were until experience
readjusted your focus like
the older customer telling

the peach-faced boy
to breathe, assuring him
that the fate of the world

won't rest solely on his shoulders,
that the lack of seating
is no sign of the Apocalypse.

The Good Meal

Do not rush a good meal like fast food.
The tongue should be something that one savors
because to be gluttonous would be rude.

At this point, sweat lines the top lip like dew
when balmy mouths learn the heat's slow labor.
Do not rush a good meal like fast food.

The kisses should be moist like honeydew
and consumed slow. Relish its rich flavors
because to be gluttonous would be rude.

It is neither a vegetable nor fruit,
but a delicacy odd as lavers.
Do not rush a good meal like fast food.

One mustn't be brash. Whatever you do
know the meal is still good if served later;
and that to be gluttonous would be rude.

So lovers, wait. Let this moment stew
in the kiss—moist, delicate vapors.
Do not rush a good meal like fast food
because to be gluttonous would be rude.

Misty Friday Morning

Heading home at 5 a.m.
under a sky as dark as
the stone of a mood ring,

wondering what color
it turns when day slides it
over her finger.
Am I any wiser now

after waking at the hour
God descends upon us
when He angled the moon

through an apartment
window and found a woman
has made herself a ring
around my body?

American City Movie Diner

That morning, clouds loofahed
the sky's massive blue back

while rainwater beaded
a glass pane like shower tile.
You smiled as if these sheen-slick

streets and wind-whipped
curtains of rain were stolen

from a movie script,
as if that moment was
adapted from a novel.

You locked your fingers with
mine as if this scene was

before the on-screen kiss,
as if we weren't in a diner
waiting to be seated.

TWO

The Dive

after Terrance Hayes

In a white-tiled kitchen,
over a plastic dish of vinegar,
my hands are divers

maneuvering pass lemon slices
that could have been lily pads
or drifting jellyfish with

their pulpy tails. Chunks
of scaled and gutted flesh
shine the way treasure

shines in a sunken chest
like the coins tourists tossed
from Caribbean cruise liners

at my father and his friends
when they were boys whose
fish bodies cut currents

for foreign currency. Dad lost
several friends overtaken
by the push and pull of water,

overtaken by a kind of god
that chooses what's kept
and what gets away.

Voyeur

Each man's pile as high
as an anthill. I'm at a cookout
in Philly. *Illadelph Halflife* blares

from a row house shaded by L
tracks. At a glance, three guys
around a kitchen table might be

mistaken as chefs picking thyme
off a stem. B can't stop smiling
when the potpourri of chocolate

and herbs rush him from an oven's
open mouth. Had I been late,
my cravings might have betrayed me

the way a woman's betrayed her. The woman
with her head wrapped like a joint.
The do-good woman

who's anything but,
after mistaking the dark bars
for what she thought was
innocent and sweet.

Take Over the World:
Pinky Speaks on Brain

It's not that I'm scatterbrained
on purpose. *Egads*, Brain
is just that—he's always been
smarter than me.

Even when we were
just two albino mice running
'round the Acme Lab

before the "change." And
with this new way of speaking,
you'd think the human need
for compassion would offset
the need to dominate everything.

But I'm just the face of this operation.

Brain, Cheney—or whatever
he likes to be called—strategizes
'bout world domination.

Sixty-five episodes of playing
the imbecile and fall guy, of us
stickin' our whiskas into others'
business and calling it foreign policy.

You think I'm OK with insults and
public humiliation? *Narf!*

Where's the micehood in that?

Think I like running this hamster wheel
of a life, knowing it's come to this?

The stupid theme song and me asking
episode after bloody episode: *Gee, Brain,*
(as if I didn't already know his response)
What do you want to do tonight?

Brain on His Friendship with Pinky

The workings of his mind
are a mystery—how he turns
complex global takeover strategies
into blunders—like America

when she gets that missionary itch.
And so what if that spazzy, beetle-
headed doofus—with his nonsensical
interjections—works my nerves

like oscillating violin strings,
that he's got the intellect of a mule hoof.
All of this pales when you consider
his unconditional loyalty.

The eager assistant whisked away
on my wavering whims of world domination.
And after 65 episodes of setbacks,
when he could have called it quits

and run off with Yakko,
Wakko and Dot,
it was Pinky who kept me
in good spirits,

our late nights at the Acme Lab
laughing at his impersonations
of President Bush and his White House
staff. He even let me lament

about Billie breaking it off
because she claimed I have
'control issues.' Besides, his antics
aren't so bad,

considering he hooked me up
with a babe like Trudie,
who despite my Napoleonic ways,

thinks my resemblance
to Orson Welles is, well...
quite becoming.

Chagrin

When security escorts a woman
back to the register, you hear
other shoppers whispering
their speculations—the alarm's

scream before plainclothes officers
flank her at the door, beckoning
to come with them.
And does it matter that

you both are among the few
African Americans in a department
store that once forced Blacks
to shop in the basement where

Jim Crow banned your elders from
the dressing rooms? Can all
the Civil Rights marches and integration
keep you from flinching

at how one of your own
is handled—the officers
jerking their suspect around,
the woman shouting

for them to take their hands
off her? And afterwards,
will anything make this right
again—the gift cards

or the cashier's apology
after waving the receipt,
explaining she forgot to
disarm the anti-theft device?

BlackBerry Speaks/Txts

so u got it bad, huh?
think u know hard times
w/ ur recession—

u w/o a job & time
2 smell da fresh air,
time 2 pick up a hobby

da way idle hands
pick me up & start
stabbing me w/ thumbs.

talk abt violated.
don't know how i feel
abt having my ball

fiddled w/. wat u
take me for, that iFreak?
da next hot thing

w/ an iBody so "touch-
friendly" u can pinch her
lush apps like—well, u get

da pic. dis life ain't e-z.
a crack on da screen
or anything else

& u get discriminated
against, u get labeled
harsh things. know where

gadgets like me end up
after da hoopla, wen
da next hot item appears

like a pop-up on ur screen?
well, it aint da afterlife.
no bon voyage of tears,

no luv-bots beaming
& txting abt what a device
it was, or how its features

were a one of a kind.
it'll just be pieces of wat
i once was in a pile

of other pieces of wat once
had a helluva run in its heyday.
still think u got it bad?

Mickey Goldmill's Pep Talk or Rocky's Trainer Gets a Poet Through NaPoWrimo

So yuh ready to t'row in da towel
wit' several rounds left?

Dat NaPo-whateva's gotcha
exhausted, lookin' for yuh footin'
like Apollo Creed's right hook
tried to rip yuh skull off yuh neck?

Well, shake it off! Ain't nuttin'
but a love tap. Yuh kiss it back—
muah. Right in da kissa.

Yuh call what yuh doin' boxin'?
Should call it ballet. Dey oughta
putcha in a leotard da way yuh dancin'
wit' dis t'ing. Gonna play possum
ev'ry time somet'ing gets da best of yuh?

Might as well pack it up.
Tell dat angel on yuh shoulder
to overnight a request upstairs
and getcha outta here.
Yuh wastin' yuh life, livin' dat way.

Look, I don't know much
'bout dis writin' t'ing, 'cept
it's sort of like fightin'.

Yuh got da talent, kid,
to be a good writer. So why
yuh comin' lightweight?

In life, if somet'ing bites yuh,
yuh bite it back wit' yuh fists.
Now, putcha gloves back on,
dammit! And flip da jab, kid.

Flip da jab!

THREE

Conundrum

Circa 2007

A decade before, my brother
and I were strapped inside the leather
belly of an Oldsmobile 88 that roared

like something feral, with speakers
coughing up bass and spitting rhymes
from Busta's first album. I don't recall
where we were headed, just that we

cruised the city with our fresh
haircuts and fragrant whispers
of Egyptian Musk behind our ears.
We thought the secret was in scented

oils, or the *abracadabra* of a barber's
clippers reducing stubborn curls to rows
of waves. What we would've given for
the answer to the riddles of women,

the *open-says-a-me* to a hidden door
in the wall they might have erected
for trespassers. And wasn't it deeper
than what our father called a "lack of game,"

when science defined pheromones
as nature's airborne love potion?
That decade, we rode
with the windows down:

the breeze a cool tongue lapping
at our sweaty foreheads,
both of us wondering
what the recipe was.

What It Is

"Good Goodness" is what Derrick
calls it. Fred says it's "The Rub,"
how lovers work at each other—

tensing in an arch, bracing
for a succession of tiny explosions.
Moist lips, interlocking legs,

blood boiling and steaming
through skin. It's laying
the rod of God on non-

believers, who switch faiths
after glimpsing nirvana
in a climax. The sore muscles—

a reminder of Fred's wisdom:
All I'm sayin', yo. Is be ready
when she put the good thigh on you.

Why I Could Never Be a Vegan

after Billy Collins

The smell of charcoal gets me
nostalgic: my childhood and
those summers my parents
were always throwing something

on the grill; our backyard crowded
with neighbors two-stepping
to Stevie Wonder, reeking of Heineken,

sweat and roasted barbecue.
I wish I was sympathetic
about animal rights, but then
I remember Birmingham, fire hoses

and what was unleashed
on protesters. What's sacred
then? Ask my mom and she'll say

I might have been
an Alvin Ailey dancer the way
I Step Hop and Run to a bubbling pot
of curry goat; or how a juicy slice

of turkey has me gripping
the roasting fork like a mic.
And why are vegetables only desirable
garnishing a plate of bleu cheese

and buffalo wings? Why does salad,
despite its dressing, seem incomplete
without chicken?

Storm

Crackle of thunder.
Lightning pulses in a vein

above the clouds. I hold you
outside of El Pollo Sabroso

while Columbia Heights roars
in the air around us, roars

like the animal of greed roaming
the streets unleashed and unmuzzled

with its collar of spikes. Sometimes
I wonder if I'm living in Revelations.

Hate masquerades as the church
with its noose and pitchfork, calling

for the first black president's head
and the politicians are Judases.

But there you are—
an on-time gospel,

a missing book of the Bible,
a courier glowing

with something divine.
Your halo's a Kangol cocked

above vanilla bean locs. You wrap
your arms around my neck,

my nerves flash like lightning
above a caravan of wind

carrying the moist scent
of what's to come.

The Invitation

Your lips were petals brushing
my neck, your hands—butterflies
roaming the valley of my chest.
This was not supposed to happen

on the third date—your car idling
on the cobblestone road;
the buzz of two rum and cokes,

a current dancing your fingers
along my inner thigh.

So where does your blame lie—

on the balladeers crooning
from every club along Fell's Point;

or the full moon against its waterworn
reflection, the luminescent mouth
of the night? Anticipation throbbing

in our bass-heavy pulses.
The eye contact,
you biting your bottom lip,
then smiling.

Horn

The more I watch the news,
the more my country resembles
a biblical city destroyed by fire;

the more I think of those
who spat on the messenger
their God sent them. At the gates

of a temple called "Beautiful,"
sat a blind man. How many of us
are him? Sometimes there's no name

for what runs the streets with
misspelled picket signs and hate
as its bullhorn. Sometimes

what's wrong with this life
could be an avalanche ready
to wipe us out. The only true Bible

might be your open arms. Your name
is a communion wafer on my tongue.
The only true psalm might be

what washes over us while
we sleep, your breath in my ears—
the sound in a shell.

Headz Up

Nate wipes down his barber chair
as if he was buffing his shiny
cranberry Lincoln—his testament

to young bloods about the importance
of investing. *Don't have to take it all*

at once. Half a pill'll keep yuh up
for three hours. Ain't got no 'S'
on my chest—and damn sure

don't run 'round with no blue tights!
But afta 65 years on this earth,

ladies still call me 'the man of steel.'
Y'all laughing, but this ain't no magic-
seeds-and-beanstalk typa story.

See that car outside?
A woman bought me that.

A Father's Advice

I've broken nearly
every Commandment
sacred to my mother.

The most important one
being fornication.

So when she asked if I
(20 years old then) was still
a virgin, I was suddenly silent.

Eyes darting from gas stove
to the almond cupboards.

How does a former junior
usher explain his list of lovers
and favorite positions,

his groping in darkened backseats
and on the sides of public buildings,

or how the orgasm, like anything
exotic, thrusts the curiosity
of those once innocent?

So I broke another Commandment
when my father's wisdom popped
into my head:

It's OK to lie sometimes, he said.
Remember the doctor's suggestions:
It's good for her blood pressure.

Spin Cycle

Warm clothes out of the dryer—
the scent hooking its aromatic
arms around my neck

the way a college girlfriend did
before a kiss in the laundromat.
And long-buried passion rises

like a serpent when Seduction
blows her snake charmer's flute.
Could this be why the sight

of a fresh line speed bags my heart
like a child's before summer break,
or why the smell of detergent

calls me like a lover
into the laundry room
before she pulled me

between her open legs?
Her warm and wet lips ready
to take my tongue.

FOUR

Blitz

Didn't have a name
for what was in the air.
Just a sun throwing its rays

around. Clouds
in a huddle. Cheering

in the distance.
1994. Deion Sanders
in a 49ers jersey,

staring down former teammates
on the Falcons. Him high stepping

an interception
into the end zone
was all a 13-year-old

knew of grace. I fought
my friends to be number 21,

not knowing
we were already marked,
that everything beyond our parents

taunted us like linebackers,
that even the sun
was a quarterback

the clouds rushed
on the field of sky.

Out of Season

Mosquitoes stick my skin
with a thirst larger than
their slim straws, leaving
tiny pyramids swelling along

the Giza Plateau of my arm.
My sweet blood keeps them
lingering the way obsession
drives a stalker's pulse.

Nature's freeloaders feeding
even after the flowers have shown
their bright blouses, then disrobed
like exotic dancers; and even after

the trees shed their green weight
with Winter coming on the back
of a chill that swoops
and spins like birds of prey.

Flurry

A big wind pushes flurries
like a cloth curtain. As a kid,
there was something enchanting

about snow—how it turned
a neighborhood into the gingerbread
towns you saw in holiday cookbooks;

when you wondered if God, in His
apron and chef's hat, sprinkled sugar
and vanilla powder

over the birch and ash trees lining
your block; or if He was responsible
for grass resembling a lawn of lime

green Jolly Rancher sticks. You rushed
outside with your tongue extended
to catch the tiny paratroopers,

unable to say what it was
you felt when what you tasted
was far from confectionery.

Composite Sketch

My man left a Tec and a nine at my crib
Turned himself in, he had to do a bid
A one-to-three, he be home the end of '93
I'm ready to get this paper, G, you with me?
                    —Biggie, "Gimme The Loot"

Thinkin' back/ reminiscing on my teens
a young G/ gettin' paid over dope fiends
fuckin' off cash that I make/ nigga,
what's tha sense of workin hard
if you never get to play
                    —2Pac, "Bury Me A G"

Today, birds doowop
on power lines the annual
song sung this time of year.

Biggie and Pac resurrect through
rhymes blaring from speakers.
I'm fresh out of the barber's chair.

Alcohol—a sting on my shape up.
From behind, I could be any
head on the barber's chart,

or another face in a lineup.
Who am I, today, leaving
the barbershop, loved

in the big arms of this season?
The breeze blows away loose hair
before the sun licks the corn husk

of my scalp. The same sun I grew
towards when I was a stalk of a boy
trying to rise above what others

might see me as.

Translation

for HT

That evening—daylight fading into
a peach sorbet-colored sky—I pumped
my legs to get you home before curfew,

wondering then what the moon
tried to tell me—sliding its light
over your bare limbs; the scent
of your sugar cookie brown skin
sweet as Cotton Candy Bubbalicious.

And what did it all mean, this drumming
in my blood, my heart opening
like the tapered head of a tulip?

That evening, when you climbed
on the back of my mountain bike, I might
have been rickshawing a dignitary the way
the hummingbird in my chest fluttered
with your arms around my waist; my body

trying to decipher this language of touch
when the closest we'd come in 3rd grade
was sipping off the same straw.

High Noon

A storm's been gathering
on the horizon for months now.
—Natalie Graham, "But, Rosa"

Clouds gallop across
the aerial frontier. 13 years old.
A cowboy with pants pockets

for gun holsters. I slingshot stones
at the heads of flowers

and do my wishbone walk
into the horizon like the heroes
in Westerns after slaying

bad guys. I could be
Don Quixote rushing

at what I think are monsters.
Friends say the real ones carry guns
and shiny badges.

Dad says my mind's loose
as rope. Might use it

to lasso the sun.
Hogtie it to a cloud stallion
and ride, and ride.

The Meek

...the angels fall from heaven
...the day the earth stands still
   —The System, "Don't Disturb This Groove"

That night, skating around
a darkened rink with several
other silhouettes, Tanya gripped
my nervous hand.

Her skin glowing from
the purple "Couples" sign
and thick pink lips popping
Bubbalicious was all
I knew of beauty

and would probably be
the only time a chunky
12-year-old would get
so close to divinity.

To think that moment
might have been the closest
I'd come to knowing a man's
frustration for obsessing
the unattainable.

But Tanya locking her
fingers with mine and smiling,
I'm convinced God grants
the meek a small taste
of their inheritance

while my cool older
cousins along the rail
grin and nod: *Yeah,
I see you, playa.*

Cosmic Girl

Six years since you've seen her
cursive print through a sundress,

when the breeze lifted
the hem to show her flexed
calves ablaze in sunlight.

Why did you ignore your friends'
warnings, even after the third
time she'd introduced herself
by another name?

Now she's Aurora Borealis—
a band of renegade stars
streaking the dark sky.

And what a way to sum up
this woman of light with fiery hair
and a glass-blown body,

a woman who quit you
cold turkey and left you
whimpering in the arms
of friends.

Weren't the signs obvious?
Her pointing heavenward
after you asked about her hometown

or when she told you
her previous name
was a number
reserved for God.

FIVE

Etiquette

AWP NYC 2008

You watch them kick and punch the air,
awkward as toddlers. A martial arts class
for beginners? No. Writers dancing
on the last night of the conference.

And could the strained expressions
mean poets struggling to break
James Brown down to iambics
while novelists are more interested
in the narrative plot of 'Funky President,'

or lack thereof? You grew up denying
your superheroes' weaknesses.
But what do you take away from the sight
of those idolized and once known as names
on book spines lining your shelf?

Literary heavyweights
reduced to babbling drifters,
or kung fu stunt artists
fighting off imaginary muggers.

A Question of Brotherhood

Peter Staudenmeyer, 21, of Saskatchewan, Canada

Loud pop and my body
tenses at what it mistakes
for a gunshot or a child
smashing an air-filled bag

between his hands. But
it's two black guys across
the street, slapping palms
before pulling each other

into an embrace. And so much
of my youth was spent with
friends navigating our way through
the wilderness of manhood—

crushing empty beer cans
against our skulls and showing
our scars, proof we were
unsuspecting victims

of childhood curiosities.
But I don't know what to call
this moment—two linebacker-
sized men in a public display

of affection, neither one
worried how others will
perceive them hugging
longer than usual.

Siegfried and Roy

Humid today and the clouds drift
like melted ice cubes in the tea-colored
sky. Could I be a tea bag steeping

in the tall heat that withers even
the street signs like flowers? Listen
to the weathermen long enough

and they start to sound like marks taken
in a street hustle with nature. Who knows
how the weather'll behave when

the seasons intrude on one another
the way the brain intrudes on the body
when endorphins are unleashed

to overthrow the kingdom of pain inside us,
or inside the brothas wincing *gotdamn!* at
Cola-colored women whose sweet scents

mingle in the breath of something wild,
what meteorologists can't quite command.
Listen to them long enough and they become

exotic entertainers, snapping their whips
before their miscues come back to bite them,
awakening that inner kingdom.

Oddity

As if each set of arms
were grown for a talent
I neglected, or for each time

I've turned down gigs
at churches. And don't God
always take a humbling

hand to those who shun
him publicly? The morning
I woke like this, I wondered

if I'd gotten myself into a whale
of a situation, like Jonah.
Now my change cup sits out

like a spare palm, like that
of the blind man outside
the gates of a temple

called "Beautiful"—only
instead of ignoring me,
people gather to watch

what must be a circus act—
no bearded ladies or fire eaters,
though; just me outside

a metro station, playing
for mere coins—one set
of hands holding an acoustic

guitar, another angling a flute
to pursed lips, and the other
rapidly smacking congas.

Prime Directive

Dean's boyish frame
was no match for Craig who
at 6 foot 5 in high school
we called Kreeg from *Star Trek*

and who we were sure
could withstand
the Vulcan nerve pinch.

But Dean figured it worked for Spock
and wasn't he cool enough to be Shaft's
extraterrestrial counterpart—
whipping on space goons
without breaking a sweat?

And didn't Spock have earthling sistas
digging his funny name, his bowl cut
and pointy ears?

Sometimes a test of strength
may seem the only way to get noticed
by a woman as fine as Uhura.

But Dean hadn't figured on being
jacked up and punched in the face.
Didn't think he'd be lying in the hall
outside the cafeteria—dazed—

waiting on the Starship, mumbling:
Captain's Log. Stardate 419973.
Severely injured. Get me back
to Starbase.

The Glow

Leroy Green found it
after beating Sho'nuff
Shogun of Harlem
and his jheri curl posse.

Eager to find it, I wanted to be
an X-Men, throwing explosive
playing cards and blowing
stuff up like Gambit,

teleporting from one
spot to the next, disappearing
into shadows like Nightcrawler
in his shiny blue fur
with just his eyes glowing.

Now I tap into that "mystical energy"
whenever I open a book. All I knew then
was that I wanted to be iridescent—
roundhousing villains without
the thought of rescuing Vanity.

Invocation

Whatever happened...?
Times done changed.
            —De La Soul, "Super Emcees"

Ten bucks got us beyond
the barricade of bouncers
into State of the Union for

Old Skool Hip Hop Fridays.
The rhythm propelled itself
around dark bodies swaying

to the current of a DJ
spinning golden era
from his vinyl looms.

That night bodies crowded
the club like records stacked
inside a milk crate

under dim lights and a ceiling
sinking like the soggy bottom
of a cardboard box

straining from the weight of what
it carried. And what carries us
when all we have is the ghost

of a memory—De La's
"Super Emcees" booming through
the pillar of speakers?

Scouting Party

for Chauncey, B, Chuck, Mekdim and
freshman year at Univ. of Maryland—College Park

Could have been Ulysses' men stranded
on the Island of the Lotus Eaters,

navigating through the labyrinth
of bass-beaten bodies grinding
to Biggie under strobe lights.
We were freshmen sneaking

into an upper classman's dorm
where liquor bottles jutted

from a sink full of ice and reefer smoke
was a snake charmed into the air.
Were we lured into the dark
by what the dark held? Its pull as mysterious

as the women and their punch bowl thighs,
or the drums that possessed us

to nod like bobblehead dolls. Neither
of us willing to be rescued
from the spell of slippery bodies
basted in blue light.

Totem

She told you what you were
after holding tight enough
to squeeze an *ohh* out of her.

Your hugs were massive—
something wild and grizzled

that functioned off instinct

and urges. And as a kid,
you couldn't understand
what lived inside the blood

of most men, or how
a woman's floral scent,

her peek of flesh,

stirred what slept so long
inside you until it rose up
on its hind legs, pawing

at the light ladled
over bare limbs.

Punch Line

Was it too late
to yank back what had
already left my lips?
There we were

in a stand-off—
your eyes could have been
razors slashing my face.
So is that what you think

of me? Your clenched fists
ready to drum my body.
Before that moment
laughter might as well

have been a salve
for an oppressive history.
I wanted us back

to kissing on your couch
and fumbling to undo
buttons on our clothes
before the comedian

and his impersonation
of a cashier at a Chinese
carryout in the hood.
What did I become

in that moment?
What hurt you most—
that the comic looked like me—
or that I laughed?

SIX

The Desired Effect

You forgot the lamppost
that lit you like a diva when
I surprised you with a bouquet
of long-stemmed white lips.

You don't recall the restaurant
where both of us laughed while
you fanned your lips bitten

by spicy curry channa.
I'll never understand what makes
a woman forget those things
and go out of her way to avoid me

on the streets as if I was
panhandling for her attention;
as if you weren't the one
who left town for a week,

came back and only called
when you needed help
rearranging furniture.

Yet when you walked past
the bookstore with a new man,
and saw me inside gawking,
you smiled.

Quasimodo in NYC

Winter yanks her breezy hem
over New York City. I beat the streets
like a mad man haunted by what rattles
in his head.

I'm a man shaken by a Gyspy woman's
loud *No* when she snatches her hand
from his. I'm a man leaving what he desires
at a hotel in Times Square.

And I might be scary the way insecurities
surface like warts, the way passersby stare
at the shame that hunches my spine.

Maybe what I need is a poem
as pretty as Esmeralda
but one willing to hold the head
of something ugly
and kiss it beautiful.

Drift

Wind swooped and cackled
when you cursed the last train
leaving the platform.

It was New Year's Day.

You spent the night before counting
down at a subway station, wishing
you'd listened to instinct and stayed

home. But what called you out

at the last minute and had you
chewing Jell-O shots at a bar
across town where confetti

spiraled like glitter inside

a snow globe? What were you
searching for among the buzzing
kazoos and party blowers

punching the air? That night

the bright streamers were serpents
curled among liquor bottles that blurred
like landscape through the windows

of a train headed to the end

of its line. You watched the lit
subway cars zigzag the night
like the Dancing Dragon

of Chinese New Year.

Green

An empty wallet
gapes from the dresser.
On the floor, pants pockets
turned out. Shrugging:
Sorry, nothing here.

You fed those lines to a beggar
outside the Chili Bowl and to a guy
who rolled up on your car
at the traffic light with a squeegee
and a spray bottle.

It's been months since you were laid off.
Now you get ransom letters instead
of benefits. Your résumés are messages
in bottles bobbing to wherever prayers
take them.

Even birds seem to cackle
and trees shake their leafy-green 'fros
as if you were a boy watching the deft
hands of a con. Opportunity—
the little white ball
under those plastic cups.

Trespasser

Should I fear the brothas gathered
on the corner? Canines glistening
like the fangs of a predator
picking up the scent of its prey

or the scent of a boy sent to the store
for butter and evaporated milk.
Mom at home cooking macaroni
and cheese. Sometimes I wonder

if she knew what waited outside,
what roamed the streets looking
for wandering kids. A guy yells
from the pack: *Lemme get a dollar,*

Lil' Man. I want to go back
to my bedroom mirror, staring down
my reflection, but I'm a lion cub
practicing his roar

the way I work my face into a look
I hope says, *Don't mess with me.*
What I hope says, *Leave me alone*
or else. A look that doesn't stop

the brotha from asking again:
Lemme get a dollar, Lil' Man.
Even the moon sneers
while a jagged horizon

wounds the sky at sunset
when the sinister wind
shoves the trees.

Rise

The worm of a poem
wiggles its way
through the soil of me.

Uncertainty circles
above like birds of prey
but I'm just a man

whose head could be
a graveyard spooked by
The Ghost of Happiness

Past. Now everywhere
I look is the face of a woman
I wanted to love;

a woman convinced
the world is shaped
like an hour glass

and who mistook where
we were for separate
points of light scattered

across a sky—dark and
cold the way the earth
might greet me

when I'm nothing
but a worm climbing
towards light despite

what waits to snatch me up;
despite what lurks, waiting
for the poem to surface.

Affairs

Every night, I'm met by a woman
with skin the color of sun-glazed honey,
her dark and thick lips open

like a sliced plum; thighs long
and curved as melons. She pops up
at 3 a.m. in a web ad and asks:

Need a girlfriend? as if all it took
was an answer to get close enough
for my tongue to snowboard down

the slope of her neck, or for lonely
hands to cup her breasts like passion fruit.
And couldn't our lives be a little kinder,

our interactions with one another
less complicated, if we were upfront
about what we wanted?

Her question as casual as a waitress
asking, *Need any dessert with that,
or more sugar for your coffee?*

Proposition

Fred picks at his batter-
fried onions, shakes his head:
She said it would never work

with me; that I know too many
women. An ex told you the same thing
before demanding you either
cut your play sisters loose or lose her

for good. And why does it always
come down to the final proposition,
as if life had a limit on possibilities?

And what happens when neither party
stops fighting the forces of arbitration?
Maybe you end up dateless on a Saturday night,
sharing appetizers with your boys

in a log cabin-style restaurant—
considering the meaning
of a talking moose head on the wall.

What's Going On

It's been years since I've heard
your voice, since we last saw
each other on a night like this:
stars hemmed to the sky

like glittery sequins on a dark
formfitting dress. Even then, I wanted
to be so many things: the cursive
script of light in your long wavy hair,

the iridescent glow glazing your
olive skin. And weren't we so determined
to keep our friendship we disregarded
the possibilities?

Driving through your old area,
each street takes me back to
that night outside the record shop—
you in the *Soul Train* line and me

wanting to be the imaginary hool-a-
hoop your hips were working. All I have
now is a missed call and your message.
I don't know what to call this current

tugging us both after so long
when I'm minutes from calling you
before a friend breaks the news
of your engagement.

How to Call It

Take the woman walking
alone down a boulevard
of lovers

or the guy seated
at a table for two
with a glass of wine

and his favorite book.
Those around them will
call it as they understand.

The two individuals
unaware of the spectacle
they've become.

As if some wind-up toy
marching into walls,
or ending up in a corner

somewhere, waiting on
the great hand of kindness
to set it straight.

I need a lot of things: lips
and fingers waking the body.
And from what?

Call it hibernation,
but never loneliness.

Tim Seibles Schools Quasimodo or Know What I'm Sayin'?

Come on, bro!

Gonna be soggy as old sneaks
'cause some woman you wanted
shrieked as if you were straight
out of a Hitchcock flick?

Gonna dye your warts blue
for a pity party when the muse
is ever-present?

Rejection's a turnstile.
Think you're the first
to go through one?

Think you're the first brotha
to hurt over a woman, to scream
your pain from life's bell towers?

You're not in Paris anymore,
and how could that Gypsy woman
not see your heart as big
as Notre Dame, that it rings loud
like bells tolling each hour?

You're at the Bowery, now.
Whole lotta tongue tyin'
to be had in here, my man.

Get a load of that one at the bar.

Can Esmeralda spill into a dress
the way that poem spills her sexy
syllables inside sequin stanzas?

85

Tell me she ain't a riddle
you bustin' your brain to solve.

If I was you, home slice,
I'd forget that silly Gypsy woman
and try to get up in some wordplay.

I'm just sayin'.

SEVEN

Advisory

Night comes fierce and icy
like the woman rolling her eyes
and snapping her head away
after catching your gaze. Even

a cashier dodged your best attempts
at getting a smile. The chill tears through
your bones like termites through wood.

And how does a man keep
from freezing when his coat
and layers of clothing betray him?
Weatherman's calling it the coldest

ever. And how does a man prepare
for such a frigid forecast when Winter's
the most fickle of her siblings?

Charmed in December

Weather warm enough to confuse
the seasons, like a man mixing up
the names of his lovers.

And a salacious vibe
pulses in the wet air—

the swoosh of wind, like a blown

kiss from glossy lips; or the laughter
of a woman with a childhood urge

to climb trees. She mistook me
for an elm, tugging at my limbs
with a smile.

Stolen

Flurries fell like shavings
from ice carvings a god might have
been toiling over when you asked:
Are you kidnapping me?

Couldn't say where
I was taking you; only that
when we arrived

you would understand.
Streetlamps glazed your lips
and I remember wishing friendship
wasn't a velvet rope between us.

A male crooner asked,
If I told you I loved you
pretty baby...would you linger

*a while today?**
Watching everything covered in white,
you called it beautiful, as if
our city was a snow globe shaken
by the hands of tourists

or as if the hands of fate
shook up the possibilities
between us.

Mark Murphy wrote the lyrics to the 1978 version of Oliver Nelson's jazz standard, "Stolen Moments."

Starlight Lounge

Blood spun and flashed

like strobes on police cruisers
whipping down back roads
at night. Street lamps slammed

their light against a moon
roof. We embraced in orange

behind sigh-blurred windows,

fumbling with your bra strap
and my zipper. You wished us
away from the brightness—back

to the dark park—pointing at stars
through an open roof.

Was the breeze trying to cool

what had sat for so long
when even The Potomac
was restless? Hand behind a head,

fingers tracing a jawline,
my body was a city on high alert.

EIGHT

Holy Day

When people love...they're relaxed
and happy and friends with all the world
      —Dudley Randall, "A Poet's Not A Jukebox"

And was that the case
with your neighbor whistling
on his way to the mailbox?

It was a Saturday—sparrows
dotted power lines

like quarter notes on a staff,
like sheet music for a ballad
that might have been playing

in his head. And weren't you
as happy once—

waking to find the sun
squinting through Venetian blinds
and blushing at what it saw,

when even the flowers were
astonished by the wind's gossip?

Those mornings you
could have been a canary with
a song in your throat.

But the road back
to that place
seems to go on

like a yellow brick trail,
the one your neighbor might

be skipping now on his way
up the driveway, to whatever waits
across the threshold.

Atonement

In a grocery aisle when
a woman from high school
approaches me and those days

slide along the projector reel
in my head—the fat jokes

and rumors about me
being gay. She says she's sorry
for what she put me through.

And is it chance that brings the past
with its head hung seeking redemption?

I once saw an old man climbing
the stone steps to church—grunting
with what looked like determination

on his face. Ask me about
forgiveness and I'll say it's

anyone wise enough to go
beyond their pain for a blessing—
the old man climbing despite

what ailed him, despite gravity
lurking and waiting to snatch him.

Cruisin'

Your hands take the wheel—
wide and round as a 45, when

Smokey cuts through static.
Cruising is made for love.
You say a month is too soon

to know what we have. But
your fingers playing in my hair
and your smile say otherwise.
Could Saturday be

a record spinning long after
the needle's worked itself

grooveless? Waxy silence
like the sound of tires grabbing
asphalt while we cruise the city

in your car. You lock your fingers
with mine, stroking my knuckle
with your thumb. The pink and purple
clouds almost make the sky seem

edible. *Baby, tonight belongs to us.*
And no matter how I try to will it

the day could never be a record
skipping, delaying the next day
when you fly out for another city.

At Selam's

for Tosin

My heart might have been
a candle the way it flickered.
We were in a club below U Street
dancing to Afrobeat.

Wanted to say those three words
that night. You painted
your face with white dots along
your nose and forehead.

All I knew of you then
could fit inside the head
of a flame. And I might've been
a lantern glowing from what
I wanted to tell you.

But those words were lost
in the roll of your hips when
you lifted your hem to the side
as if what pulsed from speakers
bared its horns before charging at us.

They were lost amongst silhouettes
knocked around by the rhythm;
lost in a room of dumb bodies
the DJ jerked like a puppet master.

That night you grinded my back into
the brick wall and took my tongue
the way a tsunami overtakes
a small boat.

That night I was haunted
by worst-case scenarios—
a needle scratching
the vinyl record,
its waxy silence.

ABOUT THE POET

Alan King is a poet and journalist living in the DC metropolitan area. He writes about art and domestic issues on his blog at http://alanwking. wordpress.com. In addition to teaching creative writing throughout the DC/ Baltimore region, he's a part-time poetry instructor at the Duke Ellington School of the Arts and the senior program director at the DC Creative Writing Workshop at Charles Hart Middle School in DC's Congress Heights neighborhood. He is also a Cave Canem fellow and VONA Alum. Alan is currently a Stonecoast MFA candidate and has been nominated for a "Best of the Net" Selection as well as a Pushcart Prize.